JANA HAUSCHILD'S
TREASURY OF
CHARTED DESIGNS

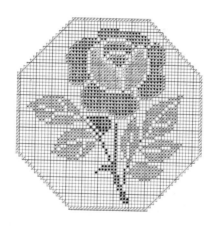

Dover Publications, Inc.

New York

Copyright © 1983 by Jana Hauschild.
All rights reserved under Pan American and International Copyright Conventions.

Published in Canada by General Publishing Company, Ltd., 30 Lesmill Road, Don Mills, Toronto, Ontario.
Published in the United Kingdom by Constable and Company, Ltd., 10 Orange Street, London WC2H 7EG.

Jana Hauschild's Treasury of Charted Designs is a new work, first published by Dover Publications, Inc., in 1983.

Manufactured in the United States of America
Dover Publications, Inc., 31 East 2nd Street, Mineola, N.Y. 11501

Library of Congress Cataloging in Publication Data

Lindberg, Jana Hauschild.
  Jana Hauschild's Treasury of charted designs.

  (Dover needlework series)
  1. Needlework—Patterns. I. Title. II. Title: Treasury of charted designs. III. Series.
TT753.L56 1983   746.44′041   83-6221
ISBN 0-486-24581-0 (pbk.)

INTRODUCTION

Jana Hauschild has long been renowned for her simple yet elegant counted cross-stitch designs. This collection of her favorite designs contains a full range of versatile and easy-to-read charts that include alphabets, flowers, children, birds, butterflies, borders and an unusual selection of allover patterns.

All of the designs are charted for ready use in different forms of needlework such as counted cross-stitch, needlepoint, latch-hooking, crochet and knitting. To give inspiration, many of the designs are shown on the covers as completed projects. You can make the items shown or use the charts to create your own needlework designs. The possibilities are as wonderful as they are endless!

Keep in mind that the finished piece of needlework will not be the same size as the charted design unless you happen to be working on fabric (or canvas) that has the same number of threads per inch as the chart has squares per inch. With knitting and crocheting, the size will vary according to the number of stitches per inch.

To determine how large a finished counted cross-stitch design will be, divide the number of stitches in the design by the thread-count of the fabric. For example, if a design that is 112 stitches wide by 140 stitches deep is worked on a 14-count cloth, divide 112 stitches by 14 to get 8 and 140 by 14 to get 10; so the worked design will measure 8″ × 10″. The same design worked on 22-count fabric would measure approximately 5″ × 6½″.

Most of these designs were originally created for counted cross-stitch; one of the great advantages to this craft is that the supplies and equipment required are minimal and inexpensive. You will need:

1. A small blunt tapestry needle, #24 or #26.
2. Evenweave fabric. This can be linen, cotton, wool or a blend that includes miracle fibers. The three most popular fabrics are:

Cotton Aida. This is made 14 threads per inch, 11 threads per inch, 8 threads per inch, and so forth. Fourteen, being the prettiest, is preferred.

Evenweave Linen. This also comes in a variety of threads per inch. Working on evenweave linen involves a slightly different technique, which is explained on page 5. Thirty-count linen will give a stitch approximately the same size as 14-count aida.

Hardanger Cloth. This has 22 threads per inch and is available in cotton or linen.
3. Embroidery thread. This can be six-strand mercerized cotton floss (DMC, Coats and Clark, Lily, Anchor, etc.), crewel wool, Danish Flower Thread, silken and metal threads or pearl cotton. DMC embroidery thread has been used to color-code all of the patterns in this book. One skein of each color given in the color key is needed, unless otherwise indicated in parentheses. For 14-count aida and 30-count linen, divide six-strand cotton floss and work with only two strands. For more texture, use more thread; for a flatter look, use less thread. Crewel wool is pretty on an evenweave wool fabric, and some embroiderers even use wool on cotton fabric. Danish Flower Thread is a thicker thread with a matte finish, one strand equaling two of cotton floss.
4. Embroidery hoop. Use a plastic or wooden 4″, 5″ or 6″ round or oval hoop with a screw type tension adjuster.
5. A pair of sharp embroidery scissors is absolutely essential.

Prepare the fabric by whipping, hemming or zigzagging on the sewing machine to prevent raveling at the edges. Next, locate the exact center of the design you have chosen, so that you can then center the design on the piece of fabric. Many of the designs in the book have an arrow at the top and along one side; follow the indicated rows to where they intersect; this is the center stitch. Next, find the center of the fabric by folding it in half both vertically and horizontally. The center stitch of the design should fall where the creases in the fabric meet.

It's usually not very convenient to begin work with the center stitch itself. As a rule it's better to start at the top of a design, working horizontal rows of a single color, left to right. This technique permits you to go from an unoccupied space to an occupied space (from an empty hole to a filled one), which makes ruffling the floss less likely. To find out where the top of the design should be placed, count squares up from the center of the design, and then count off the corresponding number of holes up from the center of the fabric.

Next, place the section of the fabric to be worked tautly

in the hoop; the tighter the better, for tension makes it easier to push the needle through the holes without piercing the fabric. As you work, use the screw adjuster to tighten as necessary. Keep the screw at the top and out of your way.

Counted cross-stitch is very simple. When beginning, fasten thread with a waste knot by holding a bit of thread on the underside of the work and anchoring it with the first few stitches (*diagram 1*). To stitch, push the threaded needle up

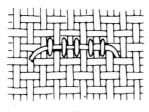

DIAGRAM 1
Reverse side of work

through a hole in the fabric and cross over the thread intersection (or square) diagonally, left to right (*diagram 2*). This

DIAGRAM 2

is half the stitch. Now cross back, right to left, making an X (*diagram 3*). Do all the stitches in the same color in the same

DIAGRAM 3

row, working left to right and slanting from bottom left to upper right (*diagram 3*). Then cross back, completing the X's (*diagram 4*). Some cross-stitchers prefer to cross each

DIAGRAM 4

stitch as they come to it; this is fine, but be sure the slant is always in the correct direction. Of course, isolated stitches must be crossed as you work them. Vertical stitches are crossed as shown in *diagram 5*. Holes are used more than

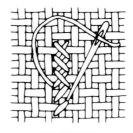

DIAGRAM 5

once; all stitches "hold hands" unless a space is indicated. The work is always held upright, never turned as for some needlepoint stitches.

When carrying a color from one area to another, wiggle your needle under existing stitches on the underside. Do not carry a color across an open expanse of fabric for more than a few stitches, as the thread will be visible from the front. Remember, in counted cross-stitch you do not work the background.

To end a color, weave in and out of the underside of stitches, perhaps making a scallop stitch or two for extra security (*diagram 6*). Whenever possible, end in the direc-

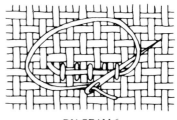

DIAGRAM 6
Reverse side of work

tion in which you are traveling, jumping up a row if necessary (*diagram 7*). This prevents holes caused by work being pulled in two directions. Do not make knots; knots make

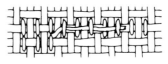

DIAGRAM 7
Reverse side of work

bumps. Cut off the ends of the threads; do not leave any tails because they'll show through when the work is mounted.

Another stitch used in counted cross-stitch is the backstitch. This is worked from hole to hole and may be vertical, horizontal or slanted (*diagram 8*).

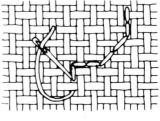

DIAGRAM 8

Working on linen requires a slightly different technique. Evenweave linen is remarkably regular, but there are always some thin threads and some that are nubbier or fatter than others. To even these out and to make a stitch that is easy to see, the cross-stitch is worked over two threads each way. The "square" you are covering is thus 4 threads (*diagram 9*). The first few stitches on linen are sometimes difficult, but one quickly begins "to see in twos." After the third stitch, a

DIAGRAM 9

pattern is established, and should you inadvertently cross over three threads instead of four, the difference in slant will make it immediately apparent that you have erred.

Linen evenweave fabric should be worked with the selvage at the side, not at the top and bottom.

Because you go over more threads, linen affords more variations in stitches. A half stitch can slant in either direction and is uncrossed. A three-fourths stitch is shown in *diagram 10. Diagram 11* shows backstitch on linen.

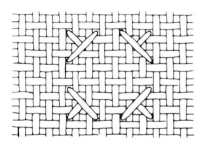

DIAGRAM 10

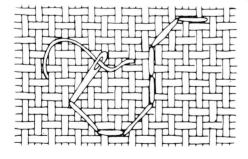

DIAGRAM 11

Gingham or other checkered material can also be used for counted cross-stitch by making the crosses over the checks from corner to corner. If you wish to embroider a cross-stitch design onto a fabric that does not have an even weave, baste a lightweight Penelope canvas to the fabric. The design can then be worked from the chart by making crosses over the double mesh of the canvas, being careful not to catch the threads of the canvas in the sewing. When the design is completed, the basting stitches are removed, and the horizontal and then the vertical threads of the canvas are removed, one strand at a time, with a tweezers. The cross-stitch design will remain on the fabric.

After you have completed your embroidery, wash it in cool or lukewarm water with a mild soap. Rinse well. Do not wring. Roll in a towel to remove excess moisture. Immediately iron on a padded surface with the embroidery face down. Be sure the embroidery is completely dry before attempting to mount it.

To mount as a picture, center the embroidery over a pure white, rag-content mat board. Turn margins over to the back evenly. Lace the margins with sturdy thread, top to bottom, side to side. The fabric should be tight and even, with a little tension. Never use glue for mounting. Counted cross-stitch on cotton or linen may be framed under glass. Wool needs to breathe and should not be framed under glass unless a breathing space is left.

Charted designs can also be used for needlepoint. The designs can be worked directly onto needlepoint canvas by counting off the correct number of warp and weft squares shown on the chart, each square representing one stitch to be taken on the canvas. If you prefer to put some guidelines on the canvas, make certain that your marking medium is waterproof. Use either nonsoluble inks, acrylic paints thinned appropriately with water so as not to clog the holes in the canvas, or oil paints mixed with benzine or turpentine. Felt-tipped pens are very handy, but check the labels carefully because not all felt markers are waterproof. It is a good idea to experiment with any writing materials on a piece of scrap canvas to make certain that all material is waterproof. There is nothing worse than having a bit of ink run onto the needlepoint as you are blocking it.

There are two distinct types of needlepoint canvas: single-mesh and double-mesh. Double-mesh is woven with two horizontal and two vertical threads forming each mesh, whereas single-mesh is woven with one vertical and one horizontal thread forming each mesh. Double-mesh is a very stable canvas on which the threads will stay securely in place as you work. Single-mesh canvas, which is more widely used, is a little easier on the eyes because the spaces are slightly larger.

A tapestry needle with a rounded, blunt tip and an elongated eye is used for needlepoint. The most commonly used needle for #10 canvas is the #18 needle. The needle should clear the hole in the canvas without spreading the threads. Special yarns that have good twist and are sufficiently heavy to cover the canvas are used for needlepoint.

Although there are over a hundred different needlepoint stitches, the Tent Stitch is universally considered to be *the* needlepoint stitch. The three most familiar versions of Tent Stitch are: Plain Half-Cross Stitch, Continental Stitch and Basket Weave Stitch.

Plain Half-Cross Stitch (*diagram 12*). Always work Half-Cross Stitch from left to right, then turn the canvas around and work the return row, still stitching from left to right. Bring the needle to the front of the canvas at a point that will be the bottom of the first stitch. The needle is in a vertical position when making the stitch. Keep the stitches loose for minimum distortion and good coverage. This stitch must be worked on a double-mesh canvas.

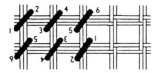

DIAGRAM 12

Continental Stitch (*diagram 13*). Start this design at the upper right-hand corner and work from right to left. The needle is slanted and always brought out a mesh ahead. The resulting stitch is actually a Half-Cross Stitch on top and a slanting stitch on the back. When the row is finished, turn the canvas around and work the return row, still stitching from right to left.

DIAGRAM 13

Basket Weave Stitch (*diagram 14*). Start in the upper right-hand corner of the area with four Continental Stitches, two worked horizontally across the top and two placed directly below the first stitch. Then work diagonal rows, the first slanting up and across the canvas from right to left and the next down and across from left to right. Each new row is

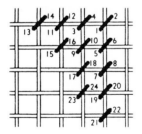

DIAGRAM 14

one stitch longer. As you go down the canvas (left to right), the needle is held in a vertical position; as you move in the opposite direction, the needle is horizontal. The rows should interlock, creating a basket-weave pattern on the reverse. If this is not done properly, a faint ridge will show where the pattern was interrupted. Always stop working in the middle of a row, rather than at the end, so that you will know in which direction you were working.

Bind all the raw edges of needlepoint canvas with masking tape, double-fold bias tape or even adhesive tape. There are no set rules on where to begin a design. Generally it is easier to begin close to the center and work outward toward the edges of the canvas, working the backgrounds or borders last. To avoid fraying the yarn, work with strands not longer than 18″.

When you have finished your needlepoint, it should be blocked. No matter how straight you have kept your work, blocking will give it a professional look.

Any hard, flat surface that you do not mind marring with nail holes and one that will not be warped by wet needle-point can serve as a blocking board. A large piece of plywood, an old drawing board or an old-fashioned doily blocker are ideal.

Moisten a Turkish towel in cold water and roll the needlepoint in the towel. Leaving the needlepoint in the towel overnight will insure that both the canvas and the yarn are thoroughly and evenly dampened. Do not saturate the needlepoint! Never hold the needlepoint under the faucet as that much water is not necessary.

Mark the desired outline on the blocking board, making sure that the corners are straight. Lay the needlepoint on the blocking board, and tack the canvas with thumbtacks spaced about ½″ to ¾″ apart. It will probably take a good deal of pulling and tugging to get the needlepoint straight, but do not be afraid of this stress. Leave the canvas on the blocking board until thoroughly dry. Never put an iron on your needlepoint. You cannot successfully block with a steam iron because the needlepoint must dry in the straightened position. You may also have needlepoint blocked professionally. If you have a pillow made, a picture framed or a chair seat mounted, the craftsman may include the blocking in the price.

Charted designs can be worked in duplicate stitch over the squares formed by stockinette stitch in knitting or afghan stitch in crochet. The patterns can also be knitted directly into the work by working with more than one color, as in Fair Isle knitting. The wool not in use is always stranded across the back of the work. When it has to be stranded over more than five stitches, it should be twisted around the wool in use on every third stitch, thus preventing long strands at the back of the work. When several colors are used, a method known as "motif knitting" is employed. In this method short lengths of wool are cut and wound on bobbins, using a separate bobbin for each color and twisting the colors where they meet to avoid gaps in the work, as in knitting argyle socks.

Most of the designs have their own color keys. The colors, however, are merely suggestions. You should feel free to substitute your own colors for the ones indicated, thereby creating a design that is uniquely yours. The designs without color keys have very simple color schemes; the selection of colors is left up to you. If you decide to create a new color scheme, work it out in detail before beginning a project. To give you a good idea of how the finished project will look, put tracing paper over the design in the book and experiment with your own colors on the tracing paper.

COLOR KEY ▶

DMC #

·		snow white
⫪	826	bright blue
⊞	352	medium peach
◩	350	dark peach
☐	676	light mustard
⊞	436	medium tan
⬕	841	dusty brown
◉	830	medium bronze
■	801	medium chocolate brown

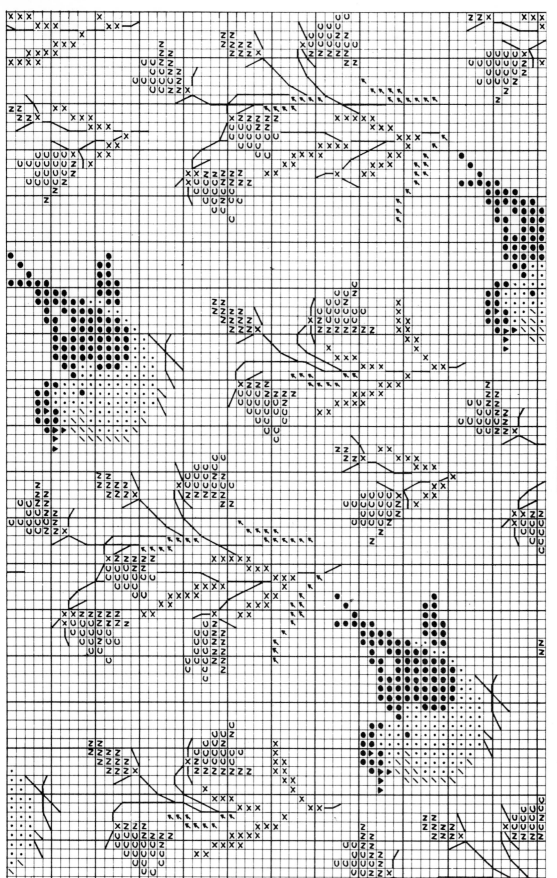

COLOR KEY

DMC #		DMC #		DMC #	
·	758 salmon	C	794 light copen blue	Z	320 medium moss green
⊠	351 medium peach	N	792 bright copen blue	X	367 bright moss green
				◉	310 black

Backstitch feet with bright tan (435); backstitch branches with bright moss green.

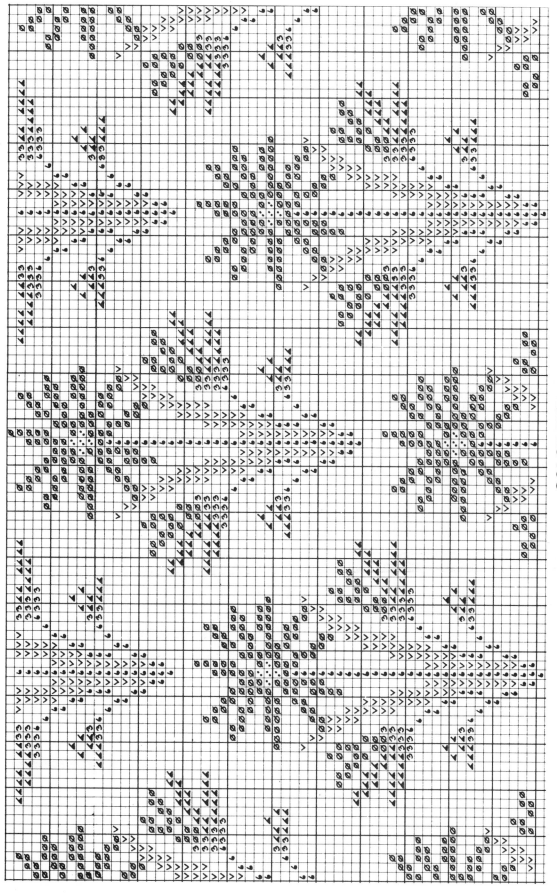

COLOR KEY

DMC #

- · 973   canary yellow
- ⊘ 899   light carnation pink

DMC #

- ◢ 309   bright carnation pink
- ▽ 471   light avocado

DMC #

- ◣ 937   dark avocado
- ▣ 433   light chocolate brown

COLOR KEY

DMC #			DMC #		
⊟	471	light avocado	◤	840	medium brown
⊠	470	medium avocado	⊞	793	medium copen blue
◣	937	dark avocado	⦿	792	bright copen blue
⧄	842	light brown	⎔	402	light copper
5	400	bright copper	■	301	medium copper

COLOR KEY

DMC #			DMC #			DMC #		
◻	725	medium marigold	◹	554	light lilac	◪	937	dark avocado
•	973	canary yellow	◪	553	medium lilac	●	3345	hunter green
◺	604	medium hot pink	⊞	3348	light spring green	◿	732	medium olive
⊞	602	light magenta	⊠	3347	medium spring green	■	434	dark tan

Backstitch branches (••••) with dark tan.

COLOR KEY

DMC #

C		snow white
·	225	powder pink
◪	224	light old rose
◤	444	dark yellow
◖	840	medium brown
⊟	989	light grass green
◪	905	bright emerald green
⊠	904	dark emerald green
●	895	hunter green

COLOR KEY

	DMC #	
⧄	726	light marigold
⊞	444	dark yellow
▯	743	dark lemon yellow
⋅	742	light yellow orange
⧅	977	golden raisin

	DMC #	
◔	972	light orange
●	729	medium mustard
⧅	794	light copen blue
⊟	318	light gray
⋅	554	light lilac

	DMC #	
⊟	553	medium lilac
▯	552	bright lilac
⧅	551	dark lilac
▯	734	pale olive
⊠	368	light moss green

	DMC #	
Ⓢ	471	light avocado
⧅	470	medium avocado
◪	937	dark avocado
■	801	medium chocolate brown

Backstitch antennae with medium chocolate brown.

COLOR KEY

	DMC #			DMC #			DMC #			DMC #	
⋅	743	dark lemon yellow	△	793	medium copen blue	⊟	552	bright lilac	⊠	436	medium tan
Ø	444	dark yellow	⊠	604	medium hot pink	⧄	472	pale avocado	●	841	dusty brown
S	783	dark marigold	‖	602	light magenta	⊞	470	medium avocado	■	839	dark brown
⊠	794	light copen blue	⫞	554	light lilac	◣	937	dark avocado			

Backstitch antennae with dark brown.

COLOR KEY ▲

DMC #

·	352	medium peach
▨	892	bright coral
▼	309	bright carnation pink
⊠	988	medium grass green
●	3345	hunter green
↗	725	medium marigold
⊡	741	medium yellow orange
◪	832	dark brass
⋁	780	dark coffee
◖	898	dark chocolate brown

Backstitch antennae with dark chocolate brown.

COLOR KEY ▶

DMC #

◪	776	medium pink
◩	962	medium strawberry
⊞	3354	light dusty pink
●	3350	dark dusty pink
·	800	light Dresden blue
⊓	472	pale avocado
⊠	470	medium avocado
■	937	dark avocado
◣	433	light chocolate brown

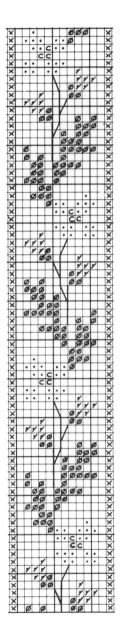
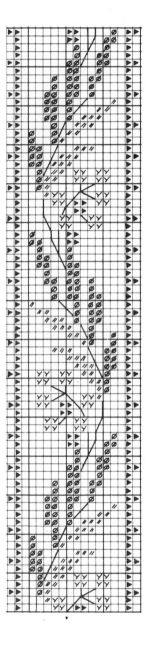

◀ **COLOR KEY**

DMC #

◹	972	light orange
•	444	dark yellow
⊠	900	dark pumpkin
◣	300	dark copper
⃝C	733	light olive
⊠	731	bright olive
⌀	3347	medium spring green
⧄	937	dark avocado

COLOR KEY ▶

DMC #

•		snow white
⊟	444	dark yellow
𝕀	742	light yellow orange
⃝O	552	bright lilac
⋀	402	light copper
◸	472	pale avocado
⊞	471	light avocado
⊠	470	medium avocado
◣	937	dark avocado
◺	731	bright olive
⬤	936	myrtle green
■	801	medium chocolate brown

18

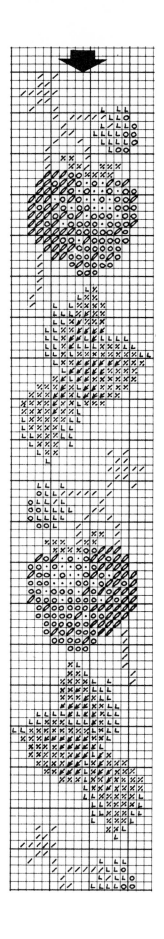

◀ COLOR KEY

DMC #

·	758	light salmon
◯	351	bright peach
⊘	350	dark peach
⧄	3013	light khaki green
⧄	3347	medium spring green
L	368	light moss green
⧄	988	medium grass green

COLOR KEY ▶

DMC #

⊠	727	pale marigold
·	726	light marigold
⧄	725	medium marigold
⊓	782	light coffee
⊞	977	golden raisin
◉	976	medium raisin
◢	437	light tan
◯	436	medium tan
■	433	light chocolate brown
⊟	3348	light spring green
⊠	3347	medium spring green
⧄	3346	dark spring green
◣	3345	hunter green

Backstitch border with medium tan.

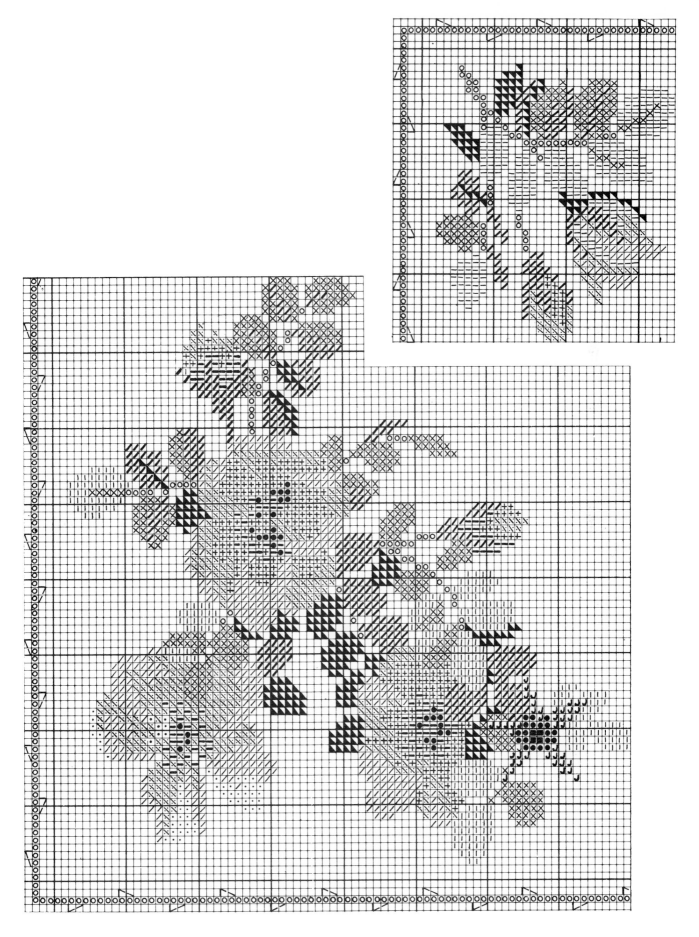

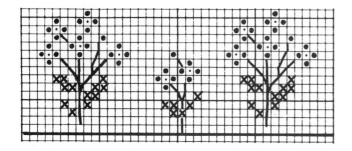

COLOR KEY

DMC #

·	972	light orange
⬤	666	scarlet
✕	906	medium emerald green

Backstitch branches with medium emerald green.

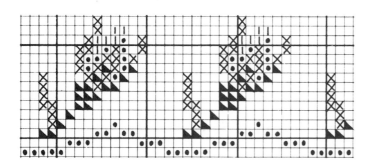

COLOR KEY

DMC #

⊞	742	light yellow orange
·	741	medium yellow orange
✕	581	light apple green
◣	731	bright olive green

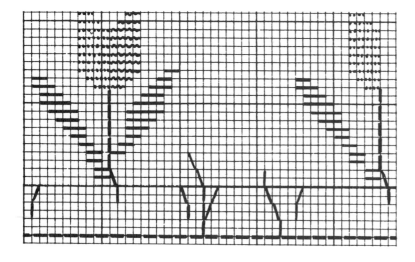

COLOR KEY

DMC #

··	893	medium coral
ᴹ	892	bright coral
⊟	906	medium emerald green

Work design in counted satin stitch for a unique effect; backstitch grass and branches with medium emerald green.

COLOR KEY

	DMC #			DMC #			DMC #	
C		snow white	▲	726	light marigold	⌀	368	light moss green
•	225	powder pink	6	436	medium tan	✕	367	bright moss green
⧄	224	light old rose	—	369	ice green	●	319	deep moss green

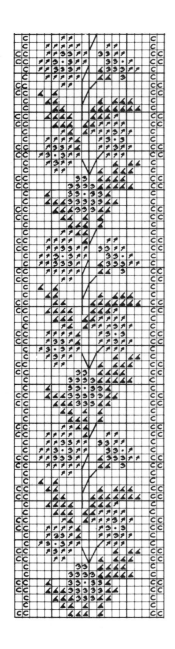 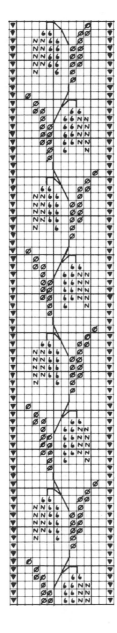

◀ COLOR KEY

DMC #

·	444	dark yellow
3	899	light carnation pink
↗	3354	light dusty pink
N	793	medium copen blue
◣	792	bright copen blue
C	733	light olive
⊘	3347	medium spring green
▲	3346	dark spring green
▼	3011	dark khaki green

Backstitch branches with dark spring green.

COLOR KEY ▶

DMC #

⊓	725	medium marigold
☒	977	golden raisin
●	976	medium raisin
⊪	729	medium mustard
⊟	554	light lilac
◩	553	medium lilac
△	3347	medium spring green
◣	469	bright avocado
⊓	3345	hunter green
■	801	medium chocolate brown

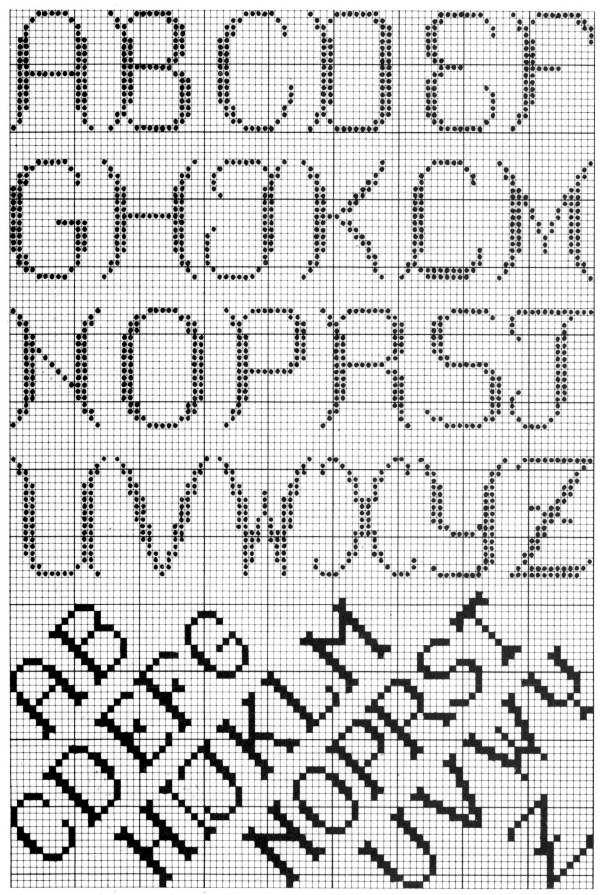

Select your own color scheme.

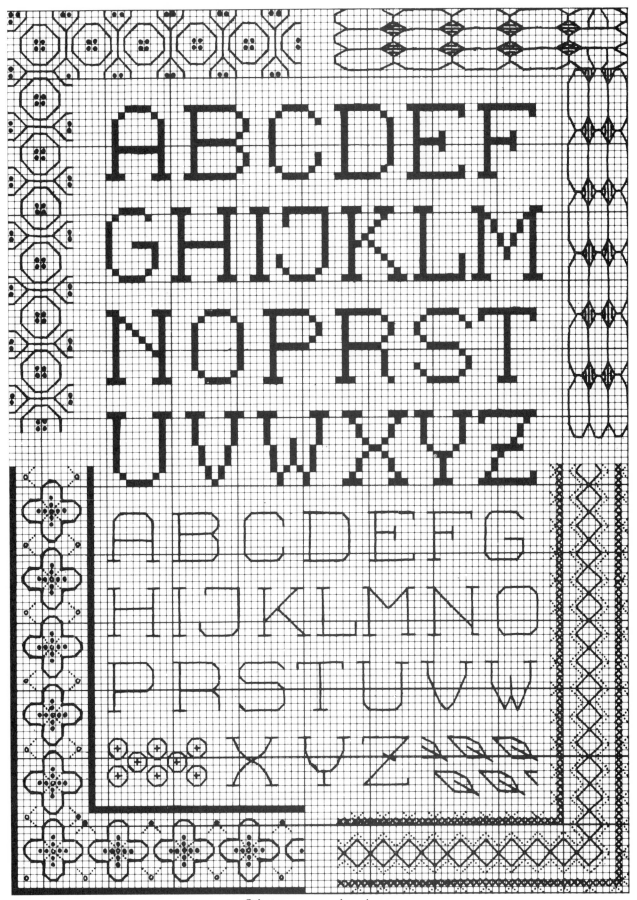

Select your own color scheme.

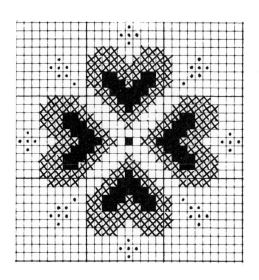

COLOR KEY

DMC #

⊡	972	light orange
⊠	608	orange red
■	666	scarlet

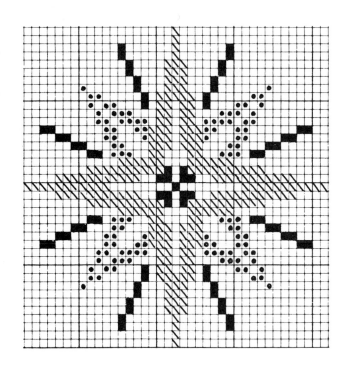

COLOR KEY

DMC #

◱	973	canary yellow
⊡	972	light orange
■	971	dark orange

Select your own color scheme.

Select your own color scheme.

Select your own color scheme.

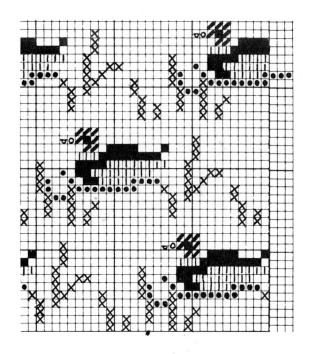

COLOR KEY

DMC #

⊡		ecru
☒	725	medium marigold
⊙	971	dark orange
⊘	701	bright kelly green
●	807	light turquoise
■	801	medium chocolate brown

At tip of beak, make a half cross-stitch (▽).

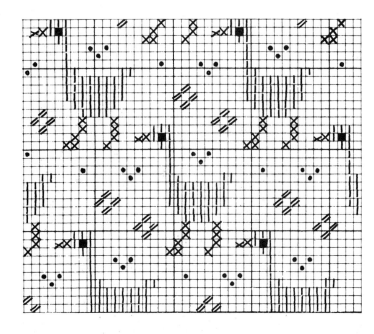

COLOR KEY

DMC #

⊡		snow white
☒	783	dark marigold
⊘	666	scarlet
⊡	797	royal blue
■	433	light chocolate brown

At tip of beak, make a half cross-stitch (✕).

COLOR KEY

DMC #

- ◹ 973 canary yellow
- ▥ 725 medium marigold
- ● 971 dark orange
- ◣ 906 medium emerald green
- ■ 310 black

At tip of beak, make a half cross-stitch (▾).

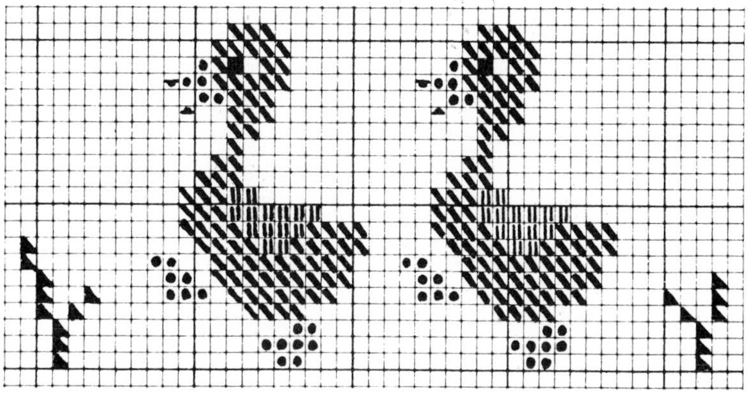

COLOR KEY

DMC #

- ⊞ 783 dark marigold
- ⊡ 434 dark tan
- ⋀ 666 scarlet
- ⧄ 927 light teal
- ⧅ 700 dark kelly green
- ■ 310 black

At tip of beak, make a half cross-stitch (⊤).

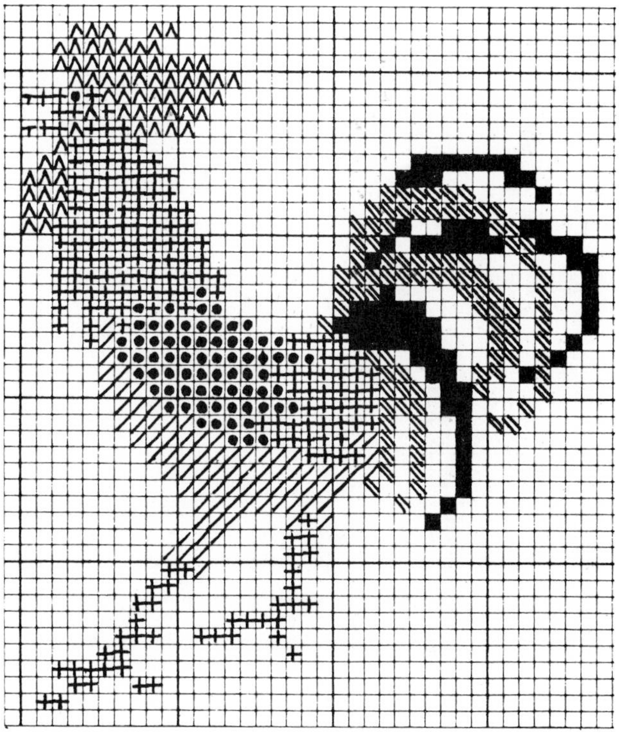

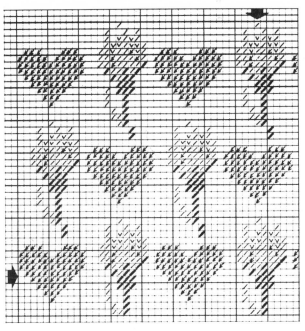

COLOR KEY

DMC #

☒	893	medium coral
☒	606	dark orange red
☒	471	light avocado
☒	937	dark avocado

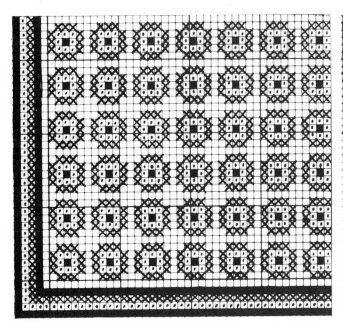

COLOR KEY

DMC #

☐	738	ice tan
⊡	554	light lilac
☒	552	bright lilac
■	3371	raw umber

COLOR KEY

DMC #

☐	3078	sunshine yellow (or ecru)
▯	437	light tan
☒	976	medium raisin
■	434	dark tan

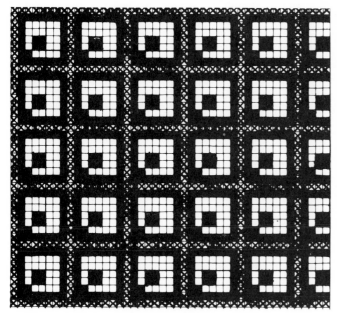

COLOR KEY

DMC #

☐ 822 ash

■ 642 coconut brown

⊠ 725 medium marigold

COLOR KEY

DMC #

☐ 740 dark yellow orange

⊠ 666 scarlet

■ 498 dark ruby

COLOR KEY

DMC #

⊡ 445 light yellow

☐ 519 medium cornflower blue

⊠ 518 bright cornflower blue

■ 930 dark soldier blue

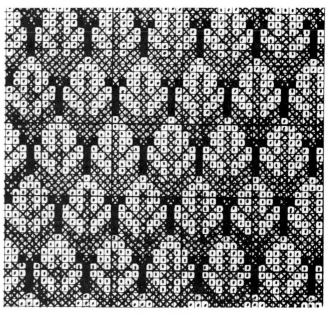

COLOR KEY

DMC #

⊡ 307 medium yellow

⊠ 834 light brass

■ 414 medium gray

◀ COLOR KEY

DMC #

⦶	973	canary yellow
⊞	725	medium marigold
Λ	793	medium copen blue
⬤	792	bright copen blue
⬕	3045	dark khaki brown
⊟	906	medium emerald green
■	434	dark tan

Backstitch branches (⋯) with medium emerald green; backstitch antennae with dark tan.

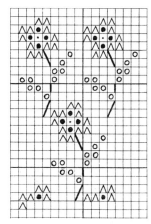

◀ COLOR KEY

DMC #

·	973	canary yellow
Λ	799	bright Dresden blue
⬤	798	dark Dresden blue
⦶	906	medium emerald green

Backstitch branches with medium emerald green.

COLOR KEY ▶

DMC #

⊘	307	medium yellow
⊠	444	dark yellow
⊘	741	medium yellow orange
·	211	light amethyst
c	210	medium amethyst
⊘	553	medium lilac
◣	552	bright lilac
③	842	light brown
⊟	3013	light khaki green
⦂	472	pale avocado
⊠	471	light avocado
⬗	469	bright avocado green
Ⅴ	320	medium moss green
⊠	987	dark grass green
⬤	935	deep hunter green

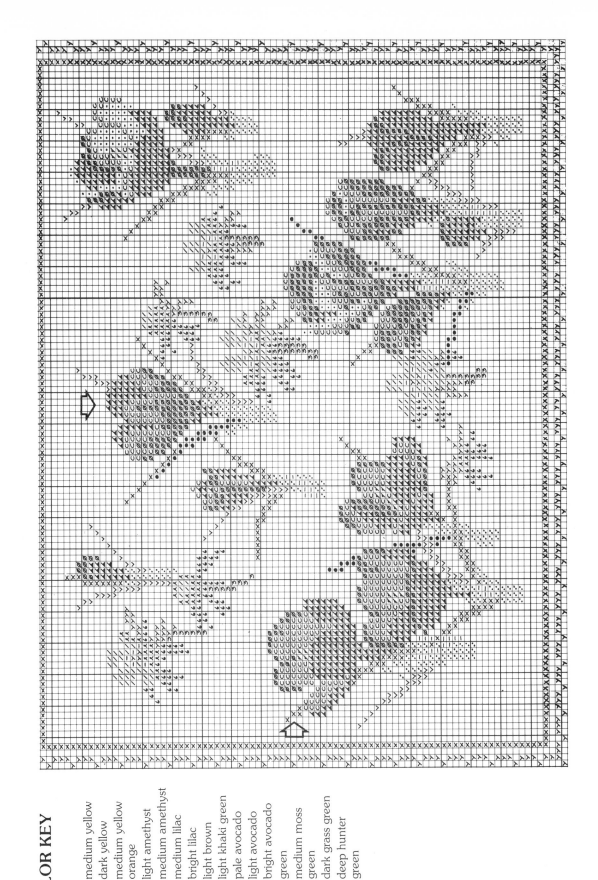

COLOR KEY

DMC #		
◹	307	medium yellow
⊠	444	dark yellow
◿	741	medium yellow orange
·	211	light amethyst
ᴄ	210	medium amethyst
⊘	553	medium lilac
◀	552	bright lilac
₃	842	light brown
‖	3013	light khaki green
⁘	472	pale avocado
◺	471	light avocado
●	469	bright avocado green
∇	320	medium moss green
⊠	987	dark grass green
●	935	deep hunter green

COLOR KEY

DMC #

⊠		ecru
⊡	822	ash
⊟	3024	pale gunmetal
⊠	318	light gray
⊡	758	light salmon
⊠	972	light orange
●	947	light pumpkin
◢	900	dark pumpkin
⊠	907	light emerald green
⊠	906	medium emerald green
⊡	987	dark grass green
⊠	922	pale sienna
⊠	921	light sienna
⊠	420	light acorn
▽	832	dark brass
⊠	839	dark brown
●	310	black

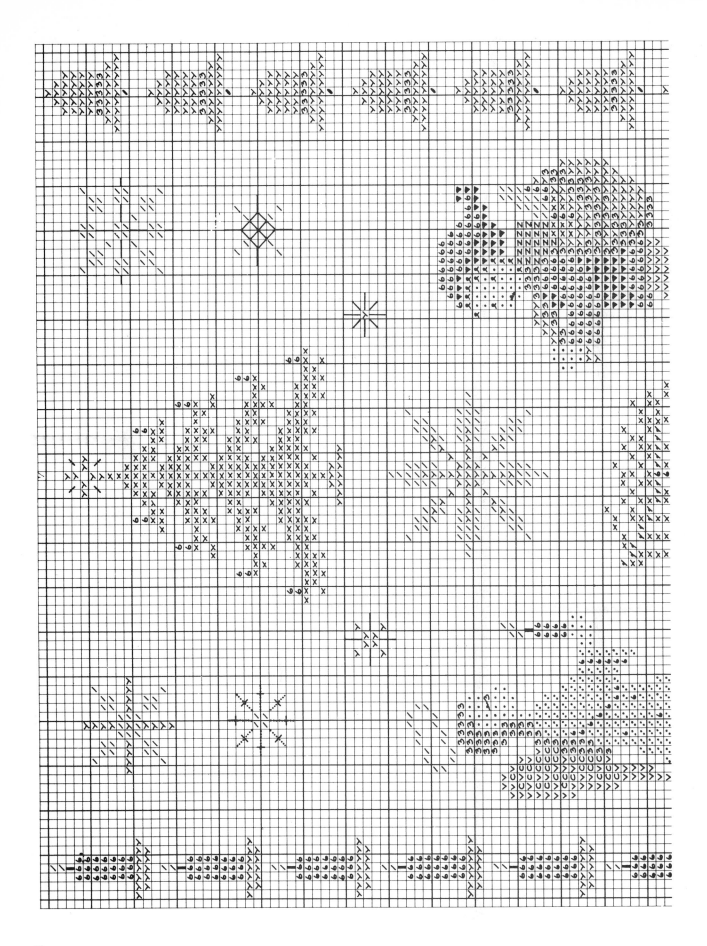

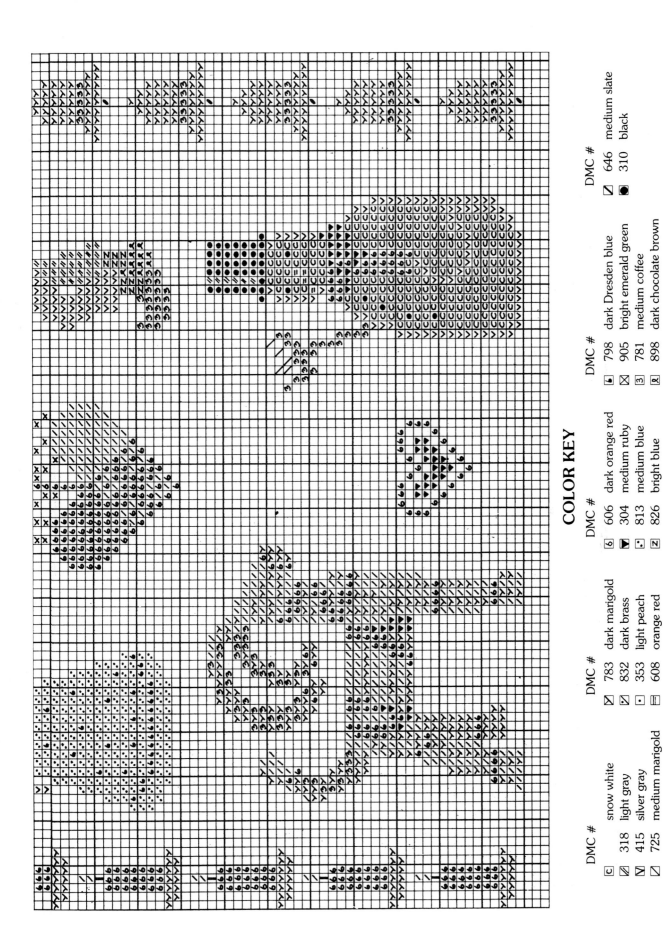

COLOR KEY

	DMC #			DMC #			DMC #			DMC #			DMC #	
ᶜ		snow white	⊠	783	dark marigold	6	606	dark orange red	▲	798	dark Dresden blue	◫	646	medium slate
◪	318	light gray	◪	832	dark brass	▶	304	medium ruby	⊠	905	bright emerald green	●	310	black
◹	415	silver gray	·	353	light peach	··	813	medium blue	③	781	medium coffee			
◿	725	medium marigold	⊞	608	orange red	◿	826	bright blue	⊠	898	dark chocolate brown			

Backstitch boy's mouth (∼) with medium ruby. Backstitch bristles on snowman's broom with medium coffee.
Backstitch candlewicks with black. Backstitch star on treetop with dark marigold.

COLOR KEY

DMC #			DMC #			DMC #		
•		snow white	⩗	946	medium pumpkin	↙	700	dark kelly green
▯	353	light peach	↓	900	dark pumpkin	⁊	731	bright olive green
⊞	352	medium peach	◖	517	dark cornflower	╱	433	light chocolate brown
╱	742	light yellow orange	⎔	702	medium kelly green	◣	310	black
⨯	741	medium yellow orange						

Backstitch mouth with scarlet (666).

COLOR KEY

	DMC #			DMC #			DMC #	
⊡	353	light peach	↓	900	dark pumpkin	⑨	731	bright olive
⊞	352	medium peach	●	517	dark cornflower	L	318	light gray
◪	742	light yellow orange	O	702	medium kelly green	◪	433	light chocolate brown
▽	946	medium pumpkin	◩	700	dark kelly green	◣	310	black

Backstitch mouth with scarlet (666); backstitch line below each eye with light chocolate brown.

COLOR KEY

DMC #

◪	783	dark marigold
⊠	972	light orange
■	349	red orange
⊡	747	light cornflower
◫	517	dark cornflower
⊞	807	light turquoise
◪	809	medium Dresden blue
⊪	798	dark Dresden blue
◉	820	dark royal blue

Backstitch hearts with red orange;
dash lines indicate center of chart
(do not embroider).

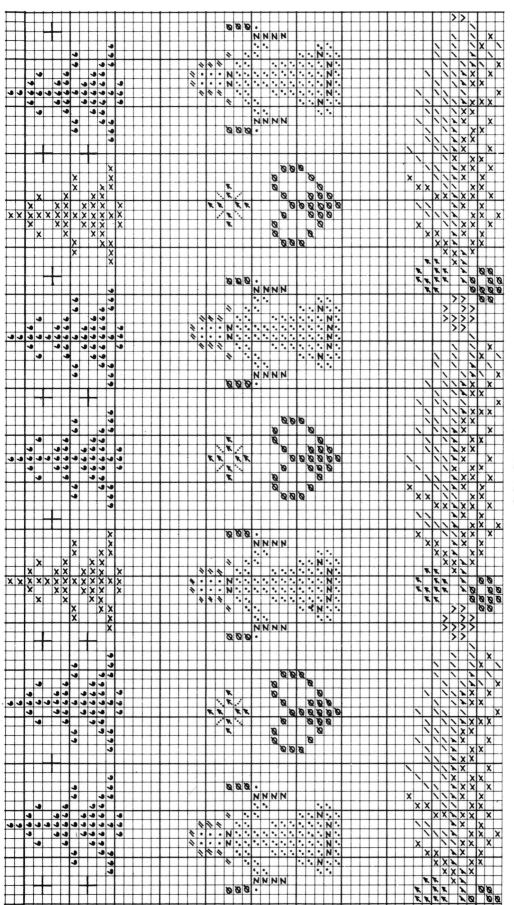

COLOR KEY

DMC #		DMC #		DMC #		DMC #	
·	754 medium flesh	◢	832 dark brass	●	304 medium ruby	◻	906 medium emerald green
◪	725 medium marigold	◩	608 orange red	·	813 medium blue	⊠	905 bright emerald green
⊠	783 dark marigold	◪	606 dark orange red	N	826 bright blue	◖	904 dark emerald green
◫	781 medium coffee						

Backstitch crosses between trees with dark marigold; backstitch stars (···) with medium marigold.

45

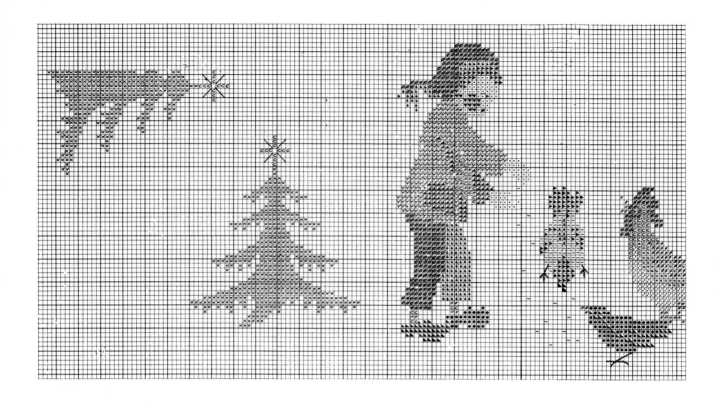

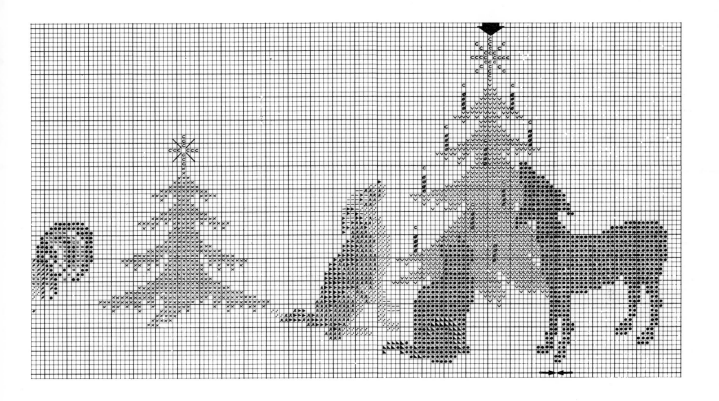

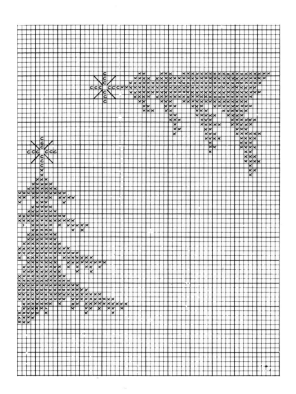

COLOR KEY

DMC #

Symbol	DMC #	Color
·	353	light peach
▼	352	medium peach
c	742	light yellow orange
⊘	971	dark orange
⊘	666	scarlet
◖	304	medium ruby
◿	794	light copen blue
⊠	825	deep blue
▲	824	dark blue
V	905	bright emerald green
✕	904	dark emerald green
⊡	437	light tan
⊟	435	bright tan
⅄	434	dark tan
↗	921	light sienna
≡	919	medium sienna
▶	801	medium chocolate brown
③	645	bright slate
◣	844	dark slate
●	310	black

Backstitch chickens' legs with dark orange; backstitch stars on treetops with light yellow orange.

COLOR KEY

DMC #

⊡	754	medium flesh
⊞	726	light marigold
S	725	medium marigold
⊠	351	bright peach
◗	666	scarlet
●	304	medium ruby
⊞	827	light blue
⊟	825	deep blue
Q	906	medium emerald green
⫼	904	dark emerald green
⧄	415	silver gray
▲	433	light chocolate brown

Backstitch children's mouths with scarlet; backstitch line below each eye with light chocolate brown; backstitch bird's beak, stars on treetops and border of design with light marigold.